D0498101

THIS CANDLEWICK BIOGRAPHY BELONGS TO:

Ramón is the biggest reason
I have gotten where I am.
He is the great one in this family.
I am still Ramón's little brother.

— PEDRO MARTÍNEZ, 1998

For William,
Caitlin, and Liam

Copyright © 2015 by Matt Tavares. All rights reserved. No part of this book may be reproduced, transmitted, or stored in an information retrieval system in any form or by any means, graphic, electronic, or mechanical, including photocopying, taping, and recording, without prior written permission from the publisher. First edition in this format 2017. Library of Congress Catalog Card Number 2014944675. ISBN 978-0-7636-6824-2 (hardcover). ISBN 978-0-7636-9310-7 (reformatted hardcover). ISBN 978-0-7636-9311-4 (paperback). This book was typeset in Agenda. The illustrations were done in watercolor, gouache, and pencil. Candlewick Press, 99 Dover Street, Somerville, Massachusetts 02144. visit us at www.candlewick.com. Printed in Shenzhen, Guangdong, China. 16 17 18 19 20 21 CCP 10 9 8 7 6 5 4 3 2 1

GROWING UP PEDRO

MATT TAVARES

CANDLEWICK PRESS

❖ TABLE OF CONTENTS ❖

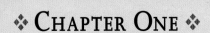

❖ Chapter One ❖

The Dominican Republic, 1981

One sunny day in the
village of Manoguayabo,
Pedro Martínez sits in the shade
and watches the older boys play.
He wants to play, too.
But his big brother, Ramón, says he is too little.
The boys are using a hard ball,
and Ramón says it's too dangerous.
Pedro is mad, but he knows
Ramón is just looking out for him.
Ramón is always looking out for Pedro.

Despite his anger, Pedro watches Ramón pitch.
He is the greatest pitcher Pedro has ever seen.

Pedro has three brothers and two sisters.
Ramón, the oldest brother,
is the baseball star of the family.

Pedro wishes he were tall, like Ramón.
He wishes he could throw hard, like Ramón.
He spends hours out behind
the little shack where they live,
throwing rocks at the mango trees.
He tries to hit only the ripe ones,
just like Ramón taught him.

Pedro loves playing baseball.
He dreams that someday
he and his brothers will play
together in the major leagues.
At night, they lie awake,
two to a mattress, and talk about what
they will do when they are millionaires.

❖ CHAPTER TWO ❖

By the time Ramón is fifteen,
he is pitching against grown men
in games around Santo Domingo.
Sometimes Pedro walks for miles
just to watch him pitch.

At sixteen, Ramón is the youngest player
on the Dominican national team.
The Los Angeles Dodgers offer him a contract.
They pay him five thousand dollars —
not much by big-league standards,
but more money than the Martínez
family has ever seen.

Ramón uses some of the money
to buy his little brother Pedro
his first real baseball glove.

In 1984, when Pedro is twelve,
Ramón starts training at Campo Las Palmas,
the Dodgers' Dominican baseball academy,
a two-hour bus ride from Manoguayabo.
Every chance he gets, Pedro tags along.

Sometimes he even gets to play catch
with Ramón on the field before practice.
For Pedro, it is like a dream.
He can't believe he is on a real baseball field
with real professional ballplayers.
He is so proud of his big brother.

One day, a coach for the Dodgers
watches Pedro pitching to Ramón.
The coach tells Pedro that if he works hard,
maybe someday the Dodgers will sign him, too.

CHAPTER THREE

In 1985, days before his seventeenth birthday,
Ramón leaves for his first season in America.
Pedro is so happy for Ramón,
but it breaks his heart to see him go.

Now that Ramón is gone,
Pedro is more determined than ever
to make it to the major leagues.
Every day, he practices and practices.

For Ramón, adjusting to life in America is not easy.
When his team stops to eat at a restaurant,
he doesn't know what to order
because all the menus are in English.
He can't talk to anyone.

Ramón tells Pedro all about it.
He wants to make sure that when it's Pedro's turn,
his little brother is ready.

Pedro keeps practicing,
and he starts studying English every day.
In 1988, when he is sixteen,
Pedro is back at Campo Las Palmas.
He is ready to try out for the Dodgers.
Dozens of other boys are trying out, too.
Most of them are much bigger
and stronger than Pedro.

He works hard and does his best.
But the Dodger scouts aren't sure.
He is still so much smaller than Ramón.
They worry that he just isn't big enough
to make it in professional baseball.

Finally, after a thirty-day tryout,
the Dodgers decide to give Pedro a chance.
They pay him six thousand, five hundred dollars.
He gives all the money to Ramón.

❖ Chapter Four ❖

In 1990, the Dodgers assign Pedro to their
minor-league team in Great Falls, Montana.
Pedro says good-bye to his family
and leaves for America.

By now, Ramón is a star in the big leagues,
the ace of the Los Angeles Dodgers.
In 1990, he wins twenty games and is the runner-up
for the National League Cy Young Award.

Some of Pedro's teammates in the minors
think Pedro is only there because he is
the great Ramón Martínez's little brother.
Pedro works hard to prove that he belongs.

He keeps working on his English, too.
During long bus rides,
he stares out the window and
tries to read every road sign.
He learns new words every day.
Before long, he can do post-game interviews
in English, without an interpreter.

Pedro races his way up through
the Dodgers' minor-league system.
Then, in September 1992,
his dream comes true.
For the first time in his life, Pedro gets to play
on the same team as his big brother.
Pedro and Ramón are in the major leagues together.

Pedro is so small and skinny
that when he arrives at Dodger Stadium,
the security guard doesn't believe
he is actually on the team.
"Hey, who are you?" he asks.
Pedro smiles. "I'm the batboy," he says.

The security guard isn't the only one
who thinks Pedro is too small.
The Dodgers' manager, Tommy Lasorda,
doesn't think Pedro is big enough
to make it as a starting pitcher.
So Pedro pitches out of the bullpen
and quickly becomes one
of the best relievers in the league.

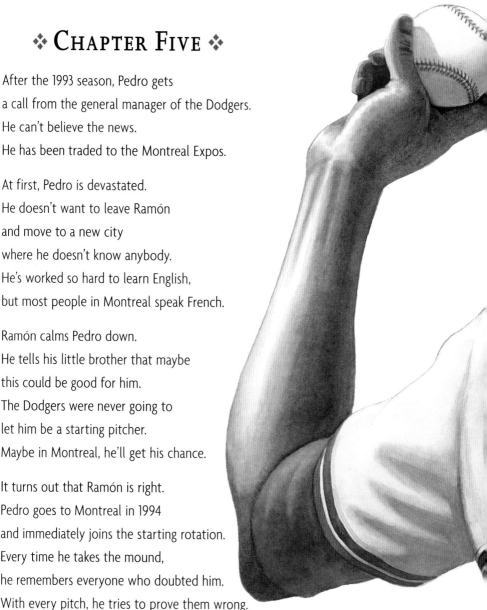

❖ Chapter Five ❖

After the 1993 season, Pedro gets
a call from the general manager of the Dodgers.
He can't believe the news.
He has been traded to the Montreal Expos.

At first, Pedro is devastated.
He doesn't want to leave Ramón
and move to a new city
where he doesn't know anybody.
He's worked so hard to learn English,
but most people in Montreal speak French.

Ramón calms Pedro down.
He tells his little brother that maybe
this could be good for him.
The Dodgers were never going to
let him be a starting pitcher.
Maybe in Montreal, he'll get his chance.

It turns out that Ramón is right.
Pedro goes to Montreal in 1994
and immediately joins the starting rotation.
Every time he takes the mound,
he remembers everyone who doubted him.
With every pitch, he tries to prove them wrong.

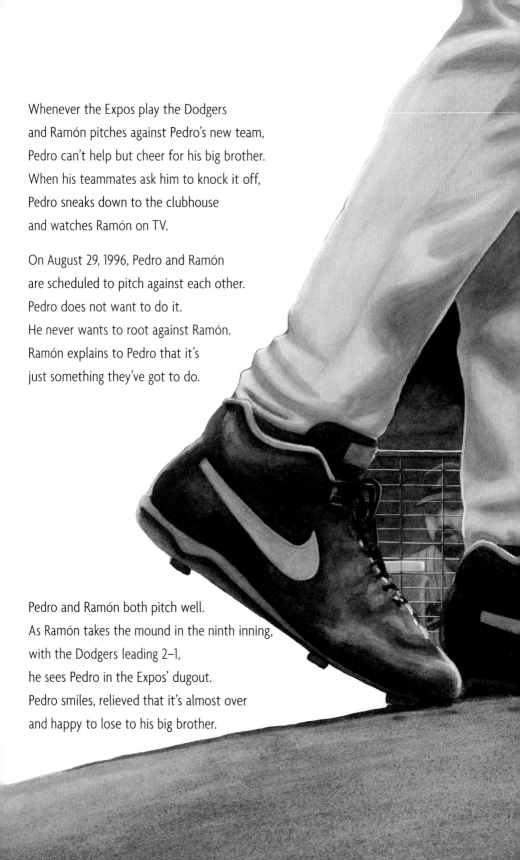

Whenever the Expos play the Dodgers
and Ramón pitches against Pedro's new team,
Pedro can't help but cheer for his big brother.
When his teammates ask him to knock it off,
Pedro sneaks down to the clubhouse
and watches Ramón on TV.

On August 29, 1996, Pedro and Ramón
are scheduled to pitch against each other.
Pedro does not want to do it.
He never wants to root against Ramón.
Ramón explains to Pedro that it's
just something they've got to do.

Pedro and Ramón both pitch well.
As Ramón takes the mound in the ninth inning,
with the Dodgers leading 2–1,
he sees Pedro in the Expos' dugout.
Pedro smiles, relieved that it's almost over
and happy to lose to his big brother.

❖ CHAPTER SIX ❖

By 1997, Pedro is the best pitcher
in the National League — even better than Ramón.
He can throw a 97-mile-per-hour fastball,
a curveball that makes hitters' knees buckle,
and a changeup that is almost impossible to hit.

Pedro is a superstar now.
The Expos know they can't afford to pay him.
So a week after he wins the
1997 National League Cy Young Award,
they trade him to the Boston Red Sox.

In December, Pedro flies to Boston
and signs a six-year, seventy-five-
million-dollar contract with the Red Sox,
making him the highest-paid baseball player of the time.

In the summer of 1998,
on days when Pedro pitches,
the streets of Boston buzz with anticipation.
By game time, Fenway Park is packed.
Fans wave Dominican flags
and chant his name:
"Pay-DRO! Pay-DRO! Pay-DRO!"

But 1998 is not a good year for Ramón.
Pitching for the Dodgers on June 14,
he tears a muscle in his shoulder.
The team doctor tells him he needs surgery.
Ramón worries that he might never pitch again.
Pedro tells his big brother not to give up.

After his operation on June 30,
Ramón spends the rest of the season working
to rebuild the strength in his injured shoulder
and watching his little brother on television.

On days when it's not his turn to pitch,
Pedro never stops talking and dancing
and laughing and joking with his teammates.
One night, to get him to settle down,
his teammates tape him to a pole in the dugout.
Pedro loves every minute of it.

But when it is his turn to pitch,
Pedro is very serious.
All day, he is quiet and focused.
When he takes the mound, he imagines
he is a lion fighting for his food.

❖ Chapter Seven ❖

In 1999, Pedro has one of the greatest
seasons any pitcher has ever had.
He wins fifteen games before the all-star break.
He's the starting pitcher in the All-Star Game
and dazzles the home crowd at Fenway Park
by striking out five of the six batters he faces.

Meanwhile, Ramón is working hard
to get back on the field.
Late in the 1999 season,
he makes it all the way back to the major leagues
and joins Pedro on the Red Sox.

During games, they sit together in the dugout.
They coach each other and help each other.
With his big brother by his side,
Pedro is better than ever.

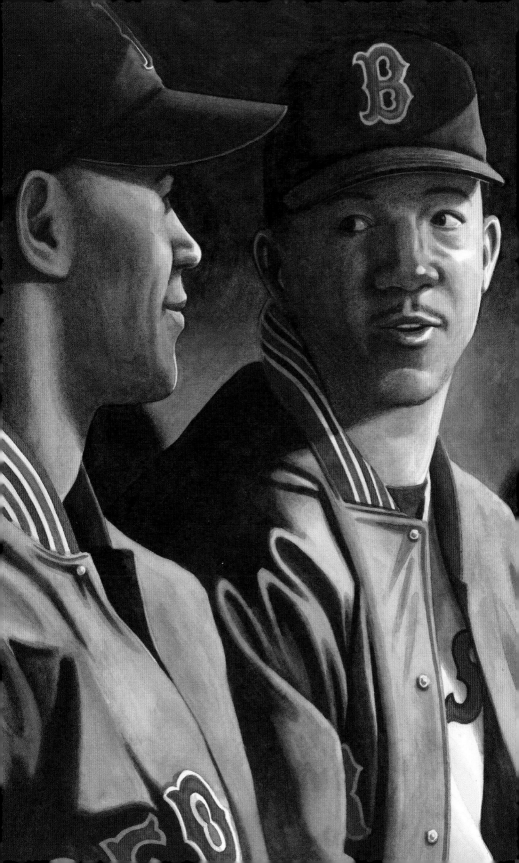

On October 9, 1999, with the Red Sox
facing elimination from the playoffs,
Ramón leads the team to victory
over the Cleveland Indians
to keep Boston's season alive.

Two days later, in the final game of the series,
Pedro's right shoulder is so sore,
he isn't supposed to pitch.
But with the score tied 8–8 in the fourth inning,
he enters the game.
Even though he can't lift his arm up
high enough to throw a good fastball,
he pitches six no-hit innings to send the Red Sox
to the American League Championship Series.

Back in the Dominican Republic,
people dance in the streets.
Kids tie scraps of metal to their bikes
and ride through the darkness.
Sparks light up the night
like fireworks.

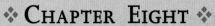

Chapter Eight

After the season,
Pedro celebrates with his family.
The little shack is gone now.
Pedro and Ramón bought all the land around it
and built this special place where
the whole family can come together.
They call it La Finca: the Little Farm.

After dinner, Pedro and Ramón walk out back
to throw rocks at the mango tree.
Together, they hit one mango after another.

Pedro hits only the ripe ones,
just like Ramón taught him.

Pedro and Ramón played together for one more season in Boston. In 2001, Ramón retired from baseball. Pedro kept on playing for the Red Sox. Every day, fans would tell him how long they had waited to see their Red Sox win the World Series. They believed that with Pedro on their team, it was finally going to happen. But every season, even with the best pitcher in baseball, the Red Sox kept falling short.

Then, in 2004, for the first time in eighty-six years, the Red Sox finally won it. The city threw a parade to celebrate, and more than three million people crowded the streets of Boston to cheer for Pedro and the Red Sox.

As a lifelong Red Sox fan, so many of my fondest baseball memories are of watching Pedro Martínez pitch. Once I spent the whole night outside Fenway Park in hopes of getting tickets to see Pedro pitch in game 3 of the 1999 American League Championship Series. When morning came, I got two tickets. I called my dad, and he joined me for the game that afternoon. Pedro did not disappoint—he struck out twelve and allowed only two hits in seven dominant innings, leading the Sox to a 13–1 victory over the Yankees.

The following spring, I sat in the upper deck at old Yankee Stadium and watched Pedro outduel Roger Clemens 2–0, in the only ball game I have ever attended where I didn't leave my seat once during the whole game because I didn't want to miss a single moment.

Pedro was a small man pitching in an era when hitters were bigger and stronger than ever. He was fearless on the mound, staring down muscle-bound sluggers and making them look like little-leaguers. Back then, I didn't know much about him beyond what I saw on the field and what I heard in his always-entertaining post-game interviews. But when I started researching his life, I learned that there was so much more to Pedro's story.

I learned about all the work he has done for the people in his hometown of Manoguayabo. When he made it to the big leagues and became a millionaire, he could have left his past behind. But he stayed in Manoguayabo and donated his time and money to help improve the lives of the people there, especially the children. He convinced the government to pave the main road. He built houses, churches, baseball fields, and a new elementary school, and he started academic programs.

Pedro Martínez overcame so many obstacles on his way to big-league stardom, from the poverty of his childhood to the fact that many people told him he was too small to succeed in the major leagues. Through it all, he worked hard and persevered and turned himself into one of the greatest pitchers of all time.

But Pedro didn't do it alone. Whenever he faced hard times along the way, it was always his big brother, Ramón, who helped him through—whether it was teaching him how to throw a curveball, encouraging him to study English, or inspiring him not to give up on his dream, even when it seemed impossible.

K—the baseball symbol for a strikeout

❖ BIBLIOGRAPHY ❖

"Brothers Glad Matchup Over: Ramón Martínez Beats Younger Brother Pedro in Rare Meeting." *Los Angeles Daily News*, August 30, 1996, p. D1.

Callahan, Gerry. "Rocket Redux." *Sports Illustrated*, April 20, 1998.

Coffey, Wayne. "Pedro the Great Really Hits Home: Friends, Family in Dominican Celebrate Victory." *New York Daily News*, October 17, 1999.

Edes, Gordon. "Brothers in Arms: The Close Relationship Between Pedro and Ramón Martínez Is Crucial to the Well-Being of Both Pitchers — and to the Fortunes of the Red Sox." *Boston Globe*, April 2, 2000, p. 12.

——. "Family Remains His Foundation." *Boston Globe*, February 6, 1998, p. D6.

——. "Pedro Martínez Climbed a Long Road to Reap Riches." *Boston Globe*, February 22, 1998.

——. "Safe at Home: Martínez Is Still an Island Wonder in Dominican Republic." *Boston Globe*, February 6, 2000, p. D1.

Gallagher, Jim. *Latinos in Baseball: Pedro Martínez*. Childs, MD: Mitchell Lane, 1999.

——. *Latinos in Baseball: Ramón Martínez*. Childs, MD: Mitchell Lane, 2000.

Gammons, Peter. "Pedro Martínez Could Throw Boston Its Best Party in a Long, Long Time." ESPN.com, January 1998.

Klein, Alan M. *Sugarball: The American Game, the Dominican Dream*. New Haven, CT: Yale University Press, 1991.

Macur, Juliet. "The Fields of Pedro's Dreams." *New York Times*, December 23, 2004.

Nightengale, Bob. "Tonight Is the Matchup Ramón and Pedro Martínez Dreaded Would Happen: Oh, Brother." *Los Angeles Times*, August 29, 1996.

Olney, Buster. "A Maestro of the Mound, Working on a Symphony." *New York Times*, July 12, 1999.

Shaughnessy, Dan. "Pedro's Effort vs. Former Team Speaks Volumes." *Boston Globe*, June 14, 2004.

Verducci, Tom. "The Power of Pedro." *Sports Illustrated*, March 27, 2000.

❖ ACKNOWLEDGMENTS ❖

I would like to thank my friends in the Dominican Republic who helped with the creation of this book: Dani Manuel Rodrigez Santana, who posed brilliantly as a young Pedro Martínez; Richy de la Cruz, who posed as Ramón and assisted in my photo sessions with Dani; Rubi Americo Guzmán, who showed me the right kind of mango trees and kindly offered to take me on a tour of the Dominican countryside on his moped; Rubi's friend Luis Brito, who took my whole family on a tour of the Dominican countryside in his car (because I was afraid to ride on the back of Rubi's moped); the family in the village of El Cupey who welcomed my family into their home; and to all the people in the Dominican Republic who talked with me about Pedro. And special thanks to Kirk Carapezza, Ryan McCarthy, Kevin McCarthy, and the K Men, as well as Cesar Sanchez; Chad Finn; Scott LaPierre; the Olin family; Ava, Molly, and Sarah Tavares; Rosemary Stimola; Kristen Nobles; and Katie Cunningham.

The epigraph on page i is taken from a January 1998 article entitled "Pedro Martínez Could Throw Boston Its Best Party in a Long, Long Time," by Peter Gammons and is used with the kind permission of ESPN.com.

❖ Pedro Martínez ❖

Height: 5 feet 11 inches; Weight: 170 lbs.;
Born: October 25, 1971, in Manoguayabo, Dominican Republic

YEAR	TEAM	W	L	ERA	G
1992	LAD	0	1	2.25	2
1993	LAD	10	5	2.61	65
1994	MON	11	5	3.42	24
1995	MON	14	10	3.51	30
1996	MON	13	10	3.70	33
1997	MON	17	8	**1.90**	31
1998	BOS	19	7	2.89	33
1999	BOS	**23**	4	**2.07**	31
2000	BOS	18	6	**1.74**	29
2001	BOS	7	3	2.39	18
2002	BOS	20	4	**2.26**	30
2003	BOS	14	4	**2.22**	29
2004	BOS	16	9	3.90	33
2005	NYM	15	8	2.82	31
2006	NYM	9	8	4.48	23
2007	NYM	3	1	2.57	5
2008	NYM	5	6	5.61	20
2009	PHI	5	1	3.63	9
18 YEARS		219	100	2.93	476

TEAMS: *LAD: Los Angeles Dodgers, MON: Montreal Expos, BOS: Boston Red Sox, NYM: New York Mets, PHI: Philadelphia Phillies*

KEY: *W: wins, L: losses, ERA: earned run average, G: games, IP: innings pitched, ER: earned runs, HR: home runs allowed, BB: walks allowed, SO: strikeouts, WHIP: walks plus hits per inning pitched, SO/BB: strikeout-to-walk ratio*

IP	ER	HR	BB	SO	WHIP	SO/BB
8.0	2	0	1	8	0.875	8.00
107.0	31	5	57	119	1.243	2.09
144.2	55	11	45	142	1.106	3.16
194.2	76	21	66	174	1.151	2.64
216.2	89	19	70	222	1.195	3.17
241.1	51	16	67	305	**0.932**	4.55
233.2	75	26	67	251	1.091	3.75
213.1	49	9	37	**313**	**0.923**	**8.46**
217.0	42	17	32	**284**	**0.737**	**8.88**
116.2	31	5	25	163	0.934	6.52
199.1	50	13	40	239	**0.923**	5.98
186.2	46	7	47	206	1.039	4.38
217.0	94	26	61	227	1.171	3.72
217.0	68	19	47	208	**0.949**	4.43
132.2	66	19	39	137	1.108	3.51
28.0	8	0	7	32	1.429	4.57
109.0	68	19	44	87	1.569	1.98
44.2	18	7	8	37	1.254	4.63
2827.1	919	239	760	3154	1.054	4.15

Boldfaced numbers indicate league-leading stats.

❖ Index ❖

MATT TAVARES is the author-illustrator of *Henry Aaron's Dream*, *There Goes Ted Williams*, and *Becoming Babe Ruth*, as well as *Zachary's Ball*, *Oliver's Game*, *Mudball*, and *Crossing Niagara*. He is the illustrator of *'Twas the Night Before Christmas*, *Over the River and Through the Wood*, *Lady Liberty* by Doreen Rappaport, *The Gingerbread Pirates* by Kristin Kladstrup, *Jubilee!* by Alicia Potter, and *Lighter than Air* by Matthew Clark Smith. Matt Tavares lives in Ogunquit, Maine.